T0022934

ASTROLOGY
SELF-CARE

Capricorn

ASTROLOGY
SELF-CARE

Capricorn

Live your best life
by the stars

Sarah Bartlett

First published in Great Britain in 2022 by Yellow Kite
An imprint of Hodder & Stoughton
An Hachette UK company

1

Illustrations © shutterstock.com

A CIP catalogue record for this title is
available from the British Library

Hardback ISBN 978 1 399 70485 4
eBook ISBN 978 1 399 70486 1
Audiobook ISBN 978 1 399 70487 8

Designed by Goldust Design

Typeset in Nocturne Serif by Hewer Text UK Ltd, Edinburgh
Printed and bound in Great Britain by Clays Ltd, Elcograf S.p.A.

Hodder & Stoughton policy is to use papers that are
natural, renewable and recyclable products and made
from wood grown in sustainable forests. The logging and
manufacturing processes are expected to conform to the
environmental regulations of the country of origin.

Yellow Kite
Hodder & Stoughton Ltd
Carmelite House
50 Victoria Embankment
London EC4Y 0DZ

www.yellowkitebooks.co.uk

I want to know what passion is.
I want to feel something strongly.

Aldous Huxley, English writer

There is a path, hidden between the road of reason and the hedgerow of dreams, which leads to the secret garden of self-knowledge. This book will show you the way.

Contents

Introduction

The ancient Greek goddess Gaia arose from Chaos and was the personification of the Earth and all of Nature. One of the first primordial beings, along with Tartarus (the Underworld), Eros (love) and Nyx (night), as mother of all life, she is both the embodiment of all that this planet is and its spiritual caretaker.

It's hardly likely you will want to become a full-time Mother Earth, but many of us right now are caring more about our beautiful planet and all that lives upon it. To nurture and respect this amazing place we call home, and to preserve this tiny dot in the Universe, the best place to start is, well, with you.

Self-care is about respecting and honouring who you are as an individual. It's about realising that nurturing yourself is neither vanity nor a conceit, but a creative act that brings an awesome sense of awareness and a deeper connection to the Universe and all that's in it. Caring about yourself means you care about everything in the cosmos – because you are part of it.

But self-care isn't just about trekking to the gym, jogging around the park or eating the right foods. It's also about discovering who you are becoming as an individual and caring for that authenticity (and loving and caring about who we are becoming means others can love and care about us, too). This is where the art of sun-sign astrology comes in.

Astrology and Self-Care

So what is astrology? And how can it direct each of us to the right self-care pathway? Put simply, astrology is the study of the planets, sun and moon and their influence on events and people here on Earth. It is an art that has been used for thousands of years to forecast world events, military and political outcomes and, more recently, financial market trends. As such, it is an invaluable tool for understanding our own individuality and how to be true to ourselves. Although there is still dispute within astrological circles as to whether the planets actually physically affect us, there is strong evidence to show that the cycles and patterns they create in the sky have a direct mirroring effect on what happens down here on Earth and, more importantly, on each individual's personality.

Your horoscope or birth-chart is a snapshot of the planets, sun and moon in the sky at the moment you were born. This amazing picture reveals all your innate potential, characteristics and qualities. In fact, it is probably the best 'selfie' you could ever have! Astrology can not only tell you who you are, but also how best to care for that self and your own specific needs and desires as revealed by your birth-chart.

Self-care is simply time to look after yourself – to restore, inspirit and refresh and love your unique self. But it's also about understanding, accepting and

11

being aware of your own traits – both the good and not so good – so that you can then say, 'It's ok to be me, and my intention is to become the best of myself'. In fact, by looking up to the stars and seeing how they reflect us down here on Earth, we can deepen our connection to the Universe for the good of all, too. Understanding that caring about ourselves is not selfish creates an awesome sense of self-acceptance and awareness.

So how does each of us honour the individual 'me' and find the right kind of rituals and practices to suit our personalities? Astrology sorts us out into the zodiac – an imaginary belt encircling the Earth divided into twelve sun signs; so, for example, what one sign finds relaxing, another may find a hassle or stressful. When it comes to physical fitness, adventurous Arians thrive on aerobic work, while soulful Pisceans feel nurtured by yoga. Financial reward or status would inspire the ambitious Capricorn mind, while theatrical Leos need to indulge their joy of being centre stage.

By knowing which sun sign you are and its associated characteristics, you will discover the right self-care routines and practices to suit you. And this unique and empowering book is here to help – with all the rituals and practices in these pages specifically suited to your sun-sign personality for nurturing and vitalising your mind, body and spirit.

However, self-care is not an excuse to be lazy and avoid the goings on in the rest of the world. Self-care is about taking responsibility for our choices and understanding our unique essence, so that we can engage with all aspects of ourselves and the way we interact with the world.

IN A NUTSHELL

Saturn, your ruler, also known as Kronos in Greek mythology, was the god of time, who ruled the 'Golden Age' of prosperity. So it's understandable that the Goat is associated with timekeeping, schedules, deadlines and having success in life. So yes, you will organise your time where work is concerned, you will meet that deadline just in time, but 'making time' to relax, chill out and care about yourself is often put off for the sake of ambition.

The practices in this little book will not only boost and care for your ambitious nature, but also give you the freedom to put aside time for your own 'Golden Age' and take time off to relax and restore your mind, body and soul.

Sun-Sign Astrology

Also known as your star sign or zodiac sign, your sun sign encompasses the following:

* Your solar identity, or sense of self
* What really matters to you
* Your future intentions
* Your sense of purpose
* Various qualities that manifest through your actions, goals, desires and the personal sense of being 'you'
* Your sense of being 'centred' – whether 'self-centred' (too much ego) or 'self-conscious' (too little ego); in other words, how you perceive who you are as an individual

In fact, the sun tells you how you can 'shine' best to become who you really are.

ASTROLOGY FACTS

The zodiac or sun signs are twelve 30-degree segments that create an imaginary belt around the Earth. The zodiac belt is also known as the ecliptic, which is the apparent path of the sun as it travels round the Earth during the year.

The sun or zodiac signs are further divided into four elements (Fire, Earth, Air and Water, denoting a certain energy ruling each sign), plus three modalities (qualities associated with how we interact with the world; these are known as Cardinal, Fixed and Mutable). So as a Capricorn, for example, you are a 'Cardinal Earth' sign.

* Fire signs: Aries, Leo, Sagittarius
  They are: extrovert, passionate, assertive

* Earth signs: Taurus, Virgo, Capricorn
  They are: practical, materialistic, sensual

* Air signs: Gemini, Libra, Aquarius
  They are: communicative, innovative, inquisitive

* Water signs: Cancer, Scorpio, Pisces
  They are: emotional, intuitive, understanding

The modalities are based on their seasonal resonance according to the northern hemisphere.

Cardinal signs instigate and initiate ideas and projects.
They are: Aries, Cancer, Libra and Capricorn

Fixed signs resolutely build and shape ideas.
They are: Taurus, Leo, Scorpio and Aquarius

Mutable signs generate creative change and adapt ideas to reach a conclusion.
They are: Gemini, Virgo, Sagittarius and Pisces

Planetary rulers

Each zodiac sign is assigned a planet, which highlights the qualities of that sign:

Aries is ruled by Mars (fearless)
Taurus is ruled by Venus (indulgent)
Gemini is ruled by Mercury (magical)
Cancer is ruled by the moon (instinctive)
Leo is ruled by the sun (empowering)
Virgo is ruled by Mercury (informative)
Libra is ruled by Venus (compassionate)
Scorpio is ruled by Pluto (passionate)
Sagittarius is ruled by Jupiter (adventurous)
Capricorn is ruled by Saturn (disciplined)
Aquarius is ruled by Uranus (innovative)
Pisces is ruled by Neptune (imaginative)

Opposite Signs

Signs oppose one another across the zodiac (i.e. those that are 180 degrees away from each other) – for example, Capricorn opposes Cancer and Taurus opposes Scorpio. We often find ourselves mysteriously attracted to our opposite signs in romantic relationships, and while the signs' traits appear to clash in this 'polarity', the essence of each is contained in the other (note, they have the same modality). Gaining insight into the characteristics of your opposite sign (which are, essentially, inherent in you) can deepen your understanding of the energetic interplay of the horoscope.

On The Cusp

Some of us are born 'on the cusp' of two signs – in other words, the day or time when the sun moved from one zodiac sign to another. If you were born at the end or beginning of the dates usually given in horoscope pages (the sun's move through one sign usually lasts approximately four weeks), you can check which sign you are by contacting a reputable astrologer (or astrology site) (see Resources, p. 117) who will calculate it exactly for you. For example, 23 August is the standardised changeover day for the sun to move into Virgo and out of Leo. But every year, the time and even sometimes the day the sun changes sign can differ. So, say you were born on 23 August at five in the morning and the sun didn't move into Virgo until five in the afternoon on that day, you would be a Leo, not a Virgo.

How To Use This Book

The book is divided into three parts, each guiding you in applying self-care to different areas of your life:

* Part One: your mind and feelings
* Part Two: your body
* Part Three: your soul

Caring about the mind using rituals or ideas tailored to your sign shows you ways to unlock stress, restore focus or widen your perception. Applying the practices in Part One will connect you to your feelings and help you to acknowledge and become aware of why your emotions are as they are and how to deal with them. This sort of emotional self-care will set you up to deal with your relationships better, enhance all forms of communication and ensure you know exactly how to ask for what you want or need, and be true to your deepest desires.

A WORD ON CHAKRAS

Eastern spiritual traditions maintain that universal energy, known as 'prana' in India and 'chi' in Chinese philosophy, flows through the body, linked by seven subtle energy centres known as chakras (Sanskrit for 'wheel'). These energies are believed to revolve or spiral around and through our bodies, vibrating at different frequencies (corresponding to seven colours of the light spectrum) in an upward, vertical direction. Specific crystals are placed on the chakras to heal, harmonise, stimulate or subdue the chakras if imbalance is found.

The seven chakras are:
*   The base or root (found at the base of the spine)
*   The sacral (mid-belly)
*   The solar plexus (between belly and chest)
*   The heart (centre of chest)
*   The throat (throat)
*   The third eye (between the eyebrows)
*   The crown (top of the head)

On p. 96 we will look in more detail at how Capricorn can work with chakras for self-care.

Fitness and caring for the body are different for all of us, too. While Capricorn benefits from muscle toning, Sagittarius prefers to go for a run, and Gemini a daily quick stretch or yoga. Delve into Part Two whenever you're in need of physical restoration or a sensual makeover tailored to your sign.

Spiritual self-care opens you to your sacred self or soul. Which is why Part Three looks at how you can nurture your soul according to your astrological sun sign. It shows you how to connect to and care for your spirituality in simple ways, such as being at one with Nature or just enjoying the world around you. It will show you how to be more positive about who you are and honour your connection to the Universe. In fact, all the rituals and practices in this section will bring you joyful relating, harmonious living and a true sense of happiness.

The Key

Remember, your birth-chart or horoscope is like the key to a treasure chest containing the most precious jewels that make you you. Learn about them, and care for them well. Use this book to polish, nurture, respect and give value to the beautiful gemstones of who you are, and, in doing so, bring your potential to life. It's your right to be true to who you are, just by virtue of being born on this planet, and therefore being a child of Mother Earth and the cosmos.

Care for you, and you care for the Universe.

CAPRICORN
WORDS OF WISDOM

As you embark on your self-care journey, it's important to look at the lunar cycles and specific astrological moments throughout the year. At those times (and, indeed, at any time you choose), the words of Capricorn wisdom below will be invaluable, empowering you with positive energy. Taking a few mindful moments at each of the four major phases of every lunar cycle and at the two important astrological moments in your solar year (see Glossary, p. 119) will affirm and enhance your positive attitude towards caring about yourself and the world.

NEW CRESCENT MOON – to care for yourself:

'Success is within my reach if I believe in me.'

'I will master my destiny because I love what I do.'

'I must learn to accept change, and not be bound by fear or duty.'

FULL MOON – for sealing your intention to care for your feeling world:

'I am responsible for my feelings and will nurture them with tenderness.'

'Being loyal to others and receiving their loyalty is the key to happiness.'

'In order to command respect, I must first respect myself.'

WANING MOON – for letting go, and letting things be:

'Failing is often part of the journey to success.'

'If the time is not right now, it soon will be, and I will know it when it arrives.'

'I will no longer follow paths; I will make my own trails.'

DARK OF THE MOON – to acknowledge your 'shadow' side:

'Being fanatical about an idea doesn't mean I have to persuade everyone to think that way, too; I can think it alone.'

'I will try not to manage the affairs of others as if they were mine.'

'I must learn to accept passion is as empowering as pragmatism.'

SOLAR RETURN SALUTATION – welcoming your new solar year to be true to who you are:

Repeat on your birthday: 'There are two kinds of people – those who see work as a mountain of impossible problems, and those who see each day as a mountain of incredible opportunities. I am the latter.'

SUN IN OPPOSITION – learn to be open to the opposite perspective that lies within you.

Repeat when the sun is in Cancer: 'My opposite sign is Cancer, a sign of empathy and the care of others. These attributes are in my birth-chart, too. I will learn to appreciate sensitivity and intuition and will be ready to listen to those who have a different way of perceiving the world.'

The Capricorn Personality

♑

Two things are infinite: the Universe and human stupidity;
and I'm not sure about the Universe.
Albert Einstein

Characteristics: Accomplished, self-sufficient, dedicated, sensual, funny, loyal, cautious, ambitious, traditional, critical, aloof, materialistic, confident, purposeful, paradoxical, serious, powerful, controlling, image-conscious, realistic, mistrustful

Symbol: the Sea Goat
In classical mythology, the constellation Capricornus was identified with a mythical being – half-goat, half-fish – and, more recently, with the mountain goat. Both symbols are used in this book for the purposes of Capricorn self-care practices.

Planetary ruler: Saturn
A gas giant, like its neighbour, Jupiter, Saturn's

extraordinarily beautiful rings are made up of thousands of smaller ringlets of ice and rock. Of the (currently) eighty-three known moons, the largest is Titan, while an array of smaller ones, known as 'shepherd moons', confine the rings and stop them from spreading out into space.

Astrological Saturn: In the birth-chart, Saturn's placement describes what we can master in life, our psychological defences, and where we compensate for our vulnerabilities. Depending on its relation to other planets in the chart, Saturn provides structure, boundaries, ambition and responsibility, so we know how to achieve our best.

Element: Earth
Like the other Earth signs, Taurus and Virgo, Capricorn is grounded in reality and skilled at managing and using resources. Earth signs are sensual, dependable and like to be in control of the material world.

Modality: Cardinal
A self-starter, Capricorn builds, initiates and organises everyone and everything, and is a visionary go-getter, who instinctively knows how to make it to the top of any chosen profession.

Body: Skeletal system (joints and knees in particular); teeth

Crystal: Ruby

Sun-sign profile: Classy, cool and controlling, Capricorn is ambitious, focused and a seriously motivated sign, and it's a rare Goat who doesn't want to succeed at something. (However, there are a few Capricorns who never aspire to the heady heights of success, due either to being overly cautious about taking any kind of risk, or to their fear of failure; if you're one of those, this book will kick-start you into thinking, Yes, actually, I can succeed.)

Often working from dawn to midnight to get to where they want to be, most Goats are determined to have everything their way and yes, money really does matter. With a tenacious desire for achievement, Capricorn can and will direct anything from films to a boardroom to win the status they seek. A goal, as long as it's realistic, gives the Goat a sense of purpose and meaning. They quickly learn the rules and codes governing social and business behaviour, such as the 'right clothes', the 'right image' and the 'right attitude' needed to achieve. And it is this traditional or calculated route to success that

29

they choose over risk or chance. Life is a serious business for the self-reliant Goat, whose instinctual wisdom gives them a powerful presence and a stylish and smart approach to living life in the success lane.

Your best-kept secret: Beneath that aloof and hard exterior is a vulnerable soul who has learned to hide their fears in wrappings of achievement or a strict work ethic.

What gives you meaning and purpose in life?
Prestige, ambition, a serious vocation, climbing to the top of your career ladder. Your solar purpose is to synthesise creativity with productivity.

What makes you feel good to be you? Status symbols, security, control, structure, maturity, style, class, classic clothes, cars, music and people, sophisticated lovers, chic perfume

What or who do you identify with? Mentors, guides, gurus, workaholics, organisations, the archetypal father figure, control freaks, the boss, historical success stories, the older generation, wisdom, orchestras, conductors

What stresses you out? Risks, the unknown, change, disorder, radical ideas, dreamers, laziness, failure, social media, doubting yourself, changing your mind, uncertainty

What relaxes you? Gardening, Nature, history books, classical music, visiting sacred places, nostalgia, browsing antique shops, collecting things, sensual massage, laughter, witty conversations, investing in property

What challenges you? Not getting your way, flighty people and their ideals, getting to the top, achievement, other people's opinions, delegating, teamwork, challenge itself

What Does Self-Care Mean For Capricorn?

Being a sophisticated, stylish Capricorn, aware of your image, you have a conventional approach to looking after yourself, with set schedules and a strong awareness of what makes you look and feel good. But for all those great intentions to get down to the nail salon before noon, if something work-related crops up, that takes precedence over cuticles and polish.

Perhaps it is the uncertainty of what all this self-care lark is really about that fazes you, rather than the actual 'doing' of it? With that in mind, this book is going to show you some wonderful ways to achieve greater self-understanding through a series of practices that won't take up much of your work time and will provide the most enriching and beneficial route to looking after you. With a few light-hearted practices and a few serious success rituals, too, you can be the best of yourself and, therefore, follow a better and happier route to achieve your goals.

Self-Care Focus

Now even a Goat needs some 'me-time' to relax and reflect on who they are and where they're going. Of course, there's nothing wrong in securing your future or chasing a realistic dream. But you'll find it easier to get to the top of your tree if you make time to review your intentions, relax your body and revive your inspiration. It may seem at odds with your strong work ethic and principles to take a day off and go for a bike ride and admire Nature, but it could lead to a brand-new insight or a way forward to achieve a goal. Don't be so involved in 'doing' or 'having' that you forget to just 'be'.

The self-care practices in this book will inspire you to 'be', and to make the best of your amazing skills, qualities and talents. They will show you how to care for and nurture the spirit of enterprise within you, to understand the vulnerable, self-doubting Goat in you and how to accomplish anything you set out to achieve, however impossible it may at first seem.

PART ONE

Caring For Your Mind And Feelings

It is never too late to be what
you might have been.

George Eliot, English novelist

This section will inspire you to delight in your thoughts, express your ideas and take pleasure in your feelings. Once you get that deep sense of awareness of who you are and what you need, not only will it feel good to be alive, but you will be even more content to be yourself. The rituals and practices here will boost your self-esteem, motivate you to lead a more serene existence and enhance all forms of relationships with others. The most important relationship of all, with yourself, will be nurtured in the best possible way according to your sun sign.

A Capricorn doesn't reach the top of the professional mountain without a lot of forethought or at least a skilled appraisal of how to be an astute social climber. Some Goats cautiously chew the cud in the lower meadows in a calculated 'wait-and-see' game, ensuring the pathway is clear of obstacles before they set off on their climb. A few others chain themselves to the railings and never make a move for fear of failure. Those who do arm themselves with the 'right equipment' (their skills) and the right weather conditions (the people, timing and places they know) are savvy enough to scale the mountain heights alone and succeed. The self-reliant and focused Capricorn is, however, often plagued by self-doubt. This stems from a fear of not being in control, and a suspicion of other people's motives. But it is often this very vulnerability that fuels their quest for power.

So whether you're a Goat who yearns for the heady heights, or one who prefers to wait and see, or even one who hasn't found their foothold yet, empowering your mind with self-belief, mettle and instinctual know-how will bring out the best in you. Caring for your mind and feelings is the best investment you can make here in the present for your long-term future.

....

THE SEA-GOAT PRACTICE

*

In most ancient texts, the symbol of Capricorn is shown as the body of a goat with a fish's tail. Babylonian astrologers identified the constellation with their god Ea (also known as Enki), who was the god of craft, water and trickery. In later Greek mythology, Capricornus was linked to Pan, the Greek god of Nature, depicted with goat horns and legs. In one myth, Pan saved himself from the monster Typhon by magically transforming his lower body and legs into a fish-tail and diving into a river.

In ancient symbolism, the Fish swims in the waters of mystery, and the Goat climbs eagerly up his mountain, his earthy senses tracking the best route to the top. And so, within you are both the organisational pragmatist and, yes, the mystic.

Here's a ritual to simultaneously home in on the achieving mountain goat and the mystical fish within you, to help you dive into the waters of inspirational thought and manifest your goals.

The timing of this is important (to reinforce the beneficial energy), so only perform this ritual on the evening of a full moon.

You will need:
* Two rough rubies (or garnets)

* An image of the symbol of Capricorn as Sea Goat
* Two small lidded jars filled with water and a drop of juniper essential oil added to each

1. Place the two rubies on the image of the Sea Goat – one on the 'tail', the other on the body.

2. With the open jars either side of the paper, say the following:

> By moonlit night empowered I'll be
> To find the way to heights of need.
> With rubies red and waters deep
> Those hidden truths will see me leap
> Upon the mountaintop of dreams
> Where all will note my high esteem.

3. Now place one ruby in each jar, put the lids on and gently shake the jars for a few moments.

4. Leave overnight, and in the morning pour off the water; let the rubies dry and then place them on your desk or in a prominent place where you can see them.

The rubies will empower you with the powerful ambition of the Goat and the mystical wisdom of the Fish in all your work.

....

CLIMB ABOARD

♡

Capricorns like to have a clear vision of their future and prefer to see it take shape before them on a daily basis. So get yourself a blackboard, pinboard or any other kind of board and make it an everyday event to review and adapt as your projects progress.

On your board, either paint, draw, stick or pin a large image of a mountain. This can be any place you like: a famous mountain, such as the breathtaking Mount Fuji, the chiselled slopes of the Matterhorn or Snowdon or the mystique of Cader Idris: the choice is yours.

When you are satisfied with your picture, stick an image (maybe a photo of yourself; or a goat) to represent you at the bottom of the mountain. Think about what you hope to achieve and how you intend to get to the top. You could write associated words in order, ascending the side of the mountain; or, again, stick or pin images of the ascent you foresee – the timescale you envisage, the ideas, costs and practicalities involved.

As you begin to map out this mountain climb, adding and subtracting things in the days or weeks ahead, the imagery will give you a true sense of direction, reminding you of the sure-footed Goat, who gets to the top and achieves what they set out to do. You might want to rearrange and adapt things, as and when your projects change. And lastly, you might choose to write this Henry Ford quote on your work board:

Failure is the opportunity to begin again more intelligently.

....

KEEP TIME

★★
★

In astrology, your ruler, the planet Saturn, embodies the qualities of determination, sagacity, stamina, purpose and discipline. The Roman god Saturn was also the god of time, and the way you organise your life reveals how important timing is to your work and progress.

Whenever you have a plan or project to initiate, set aside a few moments to practise this visualisation to ensure things fall into place at the right time.

1. Imagine a clock – maybe a grandfather clock or a quartz watch – anything that 'tells the time' and makes you happy when you gaze at it.

2. Now imagine you are competing in a cookery competition. You only have a few minutes or so to finish your dish. You still have to get your soufflé in the oven. The clock is ticking away those seconds faster than you can work your hands. Yet, as you align to the ticking and watch the clock, you realise that time is actually on your side. It's creating a structure, a framework in which to get organised. Without a good sense of timing, you might not get that soufflé risen at the right moment.

3. Now visualise the moment the challenge ends, and you are opening the oven. The soufflé is cooked to perfection.

Use this visualisation to remind you of how time is on your side, rather than against you, and it will help you to organise your life just as you'd like it to be.

....

A ROLE MODEL

✳

Many Capricorns look up to a role model, icon or someone who inspires them. This practice will remind you of what it is you aspire to, and how to use that knowledge for long-term success.

You will need:
*   A piece of paper and a pen

1. Write down at least ten genres/careers or archetypal roles you either admire or aspire to, or the names of ten famous people if you prefer.

2. The following are all traditionally associated with Capricorn:
*   Gourmet chef
*   Famous actress
*   Famous writer, artist or musician
*   Conductor of an orchestra
*   Film director
*   Organiser
*   Project manager
*   Architect
*   Magistrate
*   Creator of a fashion house or business empire

3. Now list ten ideas, qualities or subjects that inspire or matter to you. For example:

* Ancient history
* Antiques
* Ecology and preservation
* Museum conservation
* Promotion
* Prestige
* Money
* Ambition
* Business acumen
* Self-realisation

4. When you have finished your two lists, work through each of them and give every entry a value from ten down to one. Then see which role model and idea add up to the highest number when added together.

5. Working with these two together, consider how best you can combine them to make a success in the field or role in question. For example, say your two top scores were architect and business acumen – perhaps you would be best suited to running a high-profile architectural practice, rather than designing a shopping mall?

Combining the various ideas will provide food for thought, and it could be an utterly perfect new profession for you to think about. With this kind of analysis you can begin to make decisions based on the things that truly matter to you and resonate with your long-term Capricorn aspirations.

....

FREE YOURSELF

♡

Moons known as shepherd moons orbit the rings of Saturn to keep them penned in, preventing them from spiralling off into space.

In symbolic terms, those beautiful rings of Saturn represent the amazing outer image Capricorns exude as they make their way through life. But deep down inside, if you're honest with yourself, there are times when it feels as if your beautiful rings of self-esteem are, like Saturn's, being shepherded into a pen, obliged to do or achieve certain things – perhaps through family or cultural expectations. This 'pen' may also be shaped by your own fear of change.

Here's a simple way to free yourself from the 'shepherd moons' of obligation, expectation or duty.

You will need:
* 2 orange tea lights
* 2 pieces of citrine

1. Light the candles.

2. Place a stone in front of each candle and say, 'I now banish the shepherd moons of duty and obligation, for it is time to find my own true identity'.

3. Take the crystals and hold them between your hands, then blow gently on them, warming them with your breath to imbue them with your personal power.

4. Now say, 'I am free of restrictions and can go freely where I wish to go'.

5. Blow out the candles when you feel you have truly connected to and expressed your intention.

Through this practice, you will begin to establish confidence in your own desires, rather than being shepherded into a role for the sake of others. It's time to create something special for you, and you alone.

....

EMBRACING SUBTLETY

★★★

The Goat has an innate ability to see through the motives of others. (And if you're not already aware of this, then make it your intention to wake up to this potential.) Reading between the lines and taking nothing for granted means you take your time to assess a situation before you commit yourself. This is a subtle way to orchestrate others so that Capricorn is ahead of the game.

From the medieval period, the word 'subtle' has been associated with being penetrating, ingenious, refined (of the mind) and also cunning and skilled. It originates from the PIE (Proto-Indo-European) root 'teks' – 'to weave' or 'to fabricate'. According to etymologist Calvert Watkins, 'teks' was the thread that passed under the warp – considered to be the finest thread in the weave. So symbolically, the art of subtlety is Capricorn's ingenious way of weaving their way through life.

You can enhance the subtle art of being the finest thread with this little ritual.

You will need:

* 3 red tea lights
* 3 gold threads, ribbon or twine, each about 90cm (36 inches) in length

1. Light the candles and place them in a horizontal row in front of you.

2. Knot the ends of the three threads together, then begin to plait or braid them. As you make your plait, reflect on how your mind works, weaving together, fabricating and using the finest ideas to create something new, solid and workable.

3. When you have finished the braid, lay it horizontally in front of the candles.

4. Touch the braid with your finger and say, 'The warp and weft of the Universe weaves the art of subtle awareness into my mind. I am grateful for this talent and will use it wisely.'

5. Blow out the candles after a few minutes of reflecting on your ingenious mind, and leave them, along with the braid, in place overnight. Thereafter, keep the braid in a safe place.

Repeat the ritual whenever you want to amplify your ability to assess something and read between the lines.

....

THE BOLERO BUILD-UP

*

Ravel's well-known orchestral piece 'Bolero' was composed as a gradual build-up of instruments using one repetitive riff, or tune. Its powerful driving energy lies in its simplicity and, as the orchestra reaches the crescendo, it resolves with a sudden musical descent and a brilliant climax.

Once Capricorns are fired up with self-belief, they are empowered to gradually work towards the crescendo of achievement. The following exercise, which will only take about fifteen minutes, will connect the Goat to both self-belief and the spirit of entrepreneurship whenever they need a boost.

You will need:
* A recording of Ravel's 'Bolero'
* 2 rough red rubies

1. Find a quiet place where you won't be interrupted and sit and listen to the music.

2. Close your eyes, enjoy the build-up of different instruments, the structure, the plan, the arrangement.

3. Take the two rubies – one in each hand – and as the music plays, turn the stones around and around in your hands in time with the rhythm.

4. As the music dramatically ends, revel in the climactic realisation of achievement.

This practice will revive your Capricorn will to succeed.

....

WAVE A MAGIC WAND

♡

You may be a wizard of achievement when it suits you, but the one thing that's hard to magic away for Capricorn at times is negative thinking. Here's a way to banish self-doubt and negativity with, literally, a wave of a magic wand.

You will need:
* A stick, branch or any wooden rod
* A piece of paper and a pen

1. Write down on your paper one major 'negative' thought or feeling you are currently experiencing. For example, 'frustration' or 'lack of money'.

2. Place the paper about 90cm (36 inches) away from you on the ground, facing north.

3. Cast a circle around yourself with your wand in an anticlockwise direction, so that the imaginary circle creates a boundary between you and the paper.

4. Now, make a circle in the other direction and, as you do so, say, 'All negativity is outside of me. Be gone from my mind and let me be.'

5. Step outside of your magic circle and press the point of the wand into the words on the paper to disperse the feelings.

6. Tear up the paper and throw it in the bin.

After this ritual, you will feel free from all negativity.

....

BOOK BINDING

✦✦
✦

Even the most dedicated Goat has to accept that they can't do everything. As much as you think you can take on the world and organise everyone and everything in it, you have your limits. Looking after yourself, so that you can achieve to the best of your ability in life, means knowing when to stop doing all those other less important things – the ones that drain your mental and emotional energy.

Accepting you have limits will open up plenty of new opportunities that will really matter to your future. This simple practice uses the power of sealing and binding your intention to keep yourself in check.

You will need:

* A piece of paper and a pen
* A decent-sized book (one that you are not going to read again)
* A ball of string or beautiful golden thread

1. Write on the paper, 'I know when to stop, and how much I can do, and will remember to adjust accordingly'.

2. Slip the paper inside the book, between any two random pages.

3. Bind the book by winding the string around and around it, until it is completely covered.

4. Tie the string off at the ends, and as you do, say, 'I know I have boundaries and limits. I am as safely bound as this book, which protects me from overreaching myself.'

Keep the book in a place where you can see it when you work, and it will help you to know when to sit back and take a well-deserved break.

....

ACCEPTING FAILURE

✳

Even the smartest Goat can fall foul of their own grand schemes. Of course, that's rare, because you usually assess possible loss before making any kind of deal. Yet, there will be times when you might not achieve what you set out to do. Being willing to accept failure is a sign of strength, as is learning from experience and/or error.

Here's a simple way to help you realise that one failure can lead to many successes.

You will need:
* A piece of malachite
* A piece of tiger's eye
* A piece of aventurine
* 3 drops of frankincense essential oil

1. Place the crystals on a table and drizzle a tiny drop of the oil onto each one to seal your intention.

2. Say, 'There is no failure. I will either win or learn. Failure is part of success as success is part of failure.'

Leave the malachite and the tiger's eye where you can see them to support your acceptance of failure and carry the aventurine with you wherever you go to reinforce optimism.

....

MINDFUL SELF-AWARENESS

♡

Not many Capricorns have the time or inclination to enter a full meditation practice on a regular basis, whether because of a busy work schedule or simply because they don't feel it is a realistic approach to solving life's problems. However, mindfulness is a form of meditation that allows you to relax, focus and know yourself a little better. In mindfulness, you pay attention to every sensation, every breath you take, each sound you hear. This kind of practice means you can appreciate and savour the actual experience, cultivating an awareness of the beauty of life and destressing your mind.

1. Find a quiet place in the open air. This can be a park bench, a grassy hill, your own garden, an empty bus-shelter seat – anywhere you can sit just for a moment and let go of the stresses of the world.

2. You don't need to close your eyes for this, as you are going to focus on something close by. It may be the grass beneath your feet, the tree in the distance, a flower . . .

3. Gaze at your chosen object and focus on it. Just let it be as it is. As you look, you may begin to see other things in your peripheral vision and want to turn your head, but don't let your mind lead you away from your focus.

4. Be aware of the object, and of Nature and how it doesn't ask anything of you; be mindful that it is growing, changing, evolving, however slowly or quickly. This is symbolic of the 'earthiness' of Capricorn, slowly crafting and building something to call your own.

5. Come out of your mindful experience. If you continue being mindful of yourself and your actions for the rest of the day, you will be far more relaxed and ready to deal with any eventuality.

6. Whenever you are confronted with a choice, problem or challenge, focus on just being you, to relax and find stillness. Through this stillness you will find the answers you seek.

....

ATTRACTING MENTORS

★★
★

The determined Capricorn mind knows it will make its mark, in its own way. But there are times when they have no choice but to rely on helpful mentors or advisors. If you know the kinds of guide you need right now, you can use this simple ritual to attract these people into your life. If you're not sure, you can still do this practice, but leave the inner circle empty, so that whoever is right for your future plans will materialise, as if by magic.

You will need:
* A piece of paper and a pen
* 5 coins

1. Draw a large circle on your paper, with a smaller circle inside it.

2. In the small circle, write down a word or two to sum up the kind of person you're looking for. Maybe 'creative genius', 'project manager', 'tech guru' – whatever is relevant.

3. Place one of the coins over the words and the four others to the north, south, east and west, inside the bigger circle.

4. With the forefinger of your writing hand, trace a spiral on the paper from the coin in the centre in a clockwise direction, moving gradually outwards to eventually touch one of the four other coins. As you do so, visualise the type of person you are seeking. Whichever coin you touch first represents the area of life in which you will meet your mentor:

* North – financial or business associates
* South – media and social life
* East – family and known contacts
* West – creative and art worlds

Now you can use your Capricorn instinct to be on the lookout in the area of life first touched by the coin for guidance and advice.

....

POWER AND THE THRONE

✳

Now, don't get me wrong – the Goat is ambitious and wants to achieve the best for themselves, but there is this Capricorn paradox of sometimes living vicariously through other people's talents. Being the power behind the throne is safe, discreet, less risky than being on it. From behind the throne, you can organise your business colleague or loving partner to fulfil your dream.

But you need to learn how to stop pushing others to do the very thing you know *you* want to do. Here's a simple visualisation to turn vicarious living into first-hand experience, and to enjoy being the power *on* your own throne, not just behind it.

1. Visualise yourself on a chair.

2. With their back to you is someone on a throne. Without saying a word, simply move your chair in front of theirs. You are taking a gamble, but you need to make it clear you have your own throne, however modest or subtle.

3. Now imagine yourself sitting up tall, proud and serene in your chair and you will begin to experience a sense that you don't need to be the power behind anyone else's throne.

With the help of this practice, you can put yourself out there with confidence in taking a risk to manifest your dream.

Relationships

Whether in their family life, among friends or colleagues, relationships really do matter to the Goat, who needs to trust first before they give away anything about themselves. But when they do, Capricorn is probably the most loyal, true and supportive of loved ones.

Is it really all work and no play for Capricorn? Well, being serious about life means the Goat is usually serious about love, too. As cautious about forming romantic relationships as they are with business ones, they can take a long time to date or to commit. Their seduction method is usually subtle, passive and careful, while their cool aura is a shield to protect their vulnerable side. However, once the Goat has calculated all the odds, they will begin to reveal their true earthy sensuality and even their feelings.

The Goat has conventional ideas about love and sex. Traditional values – such as a good home, financial security and fidelity – matter. Capricorns also admire success. And if their partner or lover is associated with a bit of interesting history or has family connections, then so much the better. When they finally decide to mate for life, it's usually with someone who is as classy, strong-minded and ambitious for the Goat as they are for themselves.

....

THE LIGHT OF LOVE

♡

Even if Capricorns prefer work to play, there comes a time when every Goat secretly wishes for a little light romance. However, if you only spend time on building your empire, not building desire or trust in others, then love's delights are less likely to come your way. To show you're open to love (not only from others, but from yourself) activate this connection to Venus (the goddess and planet of love) every new crescent moon, until the kind of romance you seek is drawn to you.

You will need:

* A gold or white pen
* A matt black stone of any shape or type
* A Venus image (either the goddess or planet)
* 4 pieces of rose quartz
* 4 pink tea lights
* Ylang-ylang essential oil

1. With your pen, draw a heart shape on the black stone.

2. Place the stone on the Venus image.

3. Surround the image with four equally spaced rose-quartz crystals, to mark north, south, east and west.

4. Place the tea lights between these points, then light them.

5. Drop a single drop of the oil on to the black stone and say:

I welcome love from east and west,
From north and south, wherever best.
The winds they blow romance my way,
So with this breath I light my day.

6. Now blow out the candles quickly.

7. Once the flames are completely extinguished, relight the tea lights to show the Universe you are ready to light your world with love.

You can do this ritual every new crescent moon to encourage new love or indulge in a little romantic magic.

....

WORTHY OR NOT?

♡

Traditionally, the Goat isn't considered to be one of the most romantic of signs. However, deep down, beneath that cool exterior, is a soft and needy heart, ready for love – as long as there is nothing to lose and their partner is going to stick around for the long term.

To check out a new date, try this simple fun way to discover if they are worthy of your attention or not.

You will need:
* A small piece of paper and a pen

1. On your piece of paper, write down the name of the person in question.

2. Over and over and over it, and around it, in all random directions, write the two words, 'Worthy' and 'Not', until you have filled the paper with these words.

3. Now close your eyes, run your finger over and around the paper, randomly moving left, right, down, up and around in circles, until you sense intuitively the moment to stop.

4. Hold your finger very still, open your eyes and whichever word you read will tell you if this person is going to be of value to your long-term intentions.

Caring about who is worthy of your Capricorn time and any romantic investment means you can care better for yourself and your emotional needs, too.

....

TRUST

♡

Trust is hugely important for Capricorn's commitment to any relationship. The Goat can be a bit of a control freak, insisting they know the best way to run their partner's life, not forgetting trying to control friends and family, too. Capricorns need to learn to have confidence in others' decisions and choices. Here's a series of affirmations you can say to help you with this:

* I may be the conductor, but you are my first violin.
* I honour your beliefs and try not to change them.
* We share love for each other, but we are two different people, so I accept compromises have to be made.
* I listen with care to what is said – for the words spoken from the heart are to be cherished.
* I trust in what other people believe, because it is their belief, not mine.

Use the above whenever you feel you need help with trusting more and controlling less.

PART TWO

Caring For Your Body

*Every creature is a glittering,
glistening mirror of Divinity.*

Hildegard of Bingen, saint, composer and poet

Here, you will discover alternative ways to look after and nurture your body, not just as a physical presence, but its connection to mind and spirit, too. This section gives you a wide range of ideas, from using sun-sign crystals to protect your physical and psychic self to fitness, diet and beauty tips. There are specific chakra practices and yoga poses especially suited to your sun sign, not forgetting bath-time rituals and calming practices to destress you and nurture holistic wellbeing.

Like the other Earth signs, Virgo and Taurus, Capricorns are very aware of their physical needs and how to look after their health. Yet the Goat is particularly focused on achieving an immaculate image from head to toe, to give themselves outer value in their quest for achievement or fame. In fact, the Goat has the stamina and determination to be more beautiful, more physically fit, more dynamic and slicker than most other signs of the zodiac.

This section isn't going to make you stick to diet plans or fitness routines or pin you down to any rules except your own. It will simply give you a few self-care practices to help keep you trim and stay beautiful and toned from within.

Fitness and Movement

All forms of weight training, muscle toning and stretching techniques (including yoga, Pilates and tai chi) keep the Goat feeling good and looking stylish. If Capricorns are loners in the way they work (even if they have a team of professionals working with them), they are similarly loners in the world of fitness. Solo sports, such as skiing, cross-country bike riding, and solitary pursuits, like going to the gym, running a marathon and even rock climbing, suit their need to challenge themselves.

....

BREATHWORK

★★
★

With often little playtime, the Goat benefits from breathing exercises to restore balance, positivity and a harmonious energy flow. In breathwork, you exhale to release negative thoughts, beliefs or actions and also to let go of stress or anxiety. Then, when you breathe in, you take in positive energy, which not only aids circulation and builds muscle strength, but gives you the feelgood factor, too.

Here's a simple breathing exercise to help you destress, reduce tension in back muscles (often a problem for the working Goat) and restore equilibrium.

You will need:
* A drop of rose essential oil (diluted in 5 drops of sweet almond oil)

1. Drip one or two drops of the combined oil on the back of your hand (if not allergic) or just leave the oil phial open, so you can take in the scent.

2. Sit quietly and focus on the aroma as it drifts around you.

3. As you breathe in to a count of 7, be aware of the scent, as you fill your lungs right down to the base of your diaphragm, and of how this brings calmness to your mind.

4. Now breathe out slowly to the count of 11.

5. Continue in this way for at least 10 rounds of breathing, until you feel relaxed and calm, the rose scent infusing you with complete tranquillity and harmonious energy.

This breathing exercise can be done for a few minutes during busy work days or before you embark on your next Capricorn challenge.

YOGA

If you haven't tried out yoga already, this is your chance to roll out a mat, surround yourself with some atmospheric incense, candles and your favourite crystals and indulge in the sensations of suppleness, stretch and strength.

The mountain

This is probably the most basic of yoga poses, yet it still has to be technically mastered to achieve the toning and balance of spine, hips and knees. You can do this as part of a regular yoga routine or just as a standalone pose whenever you feel in need of a break, if you're hard at work all day.

1. Stand up tall, back straight and shoulders relaxed down your back.

2. With feet together, feeling your weight balanced between both feet and bottom tucked in, lift the muscles of your belly, and don't forget to lift the thigh muscles above your knees. Your arms should rest naturally by your sides, palms facing forwards.

3. With your neck straight, look forwards, into the distance.

4. Hold the pose for a minute or two and imagine you are rooted to the Earth through your feet, rising tall above it like a perfect mountain.

After practising this pose, you will feel energised and ready for the tasks ahead.

STAIRWAY TO FITNESS

Every Goat knows that reaching the top of any mountain requires stamina and effort. With that in mind, and knowing that you are naturally blessed with both, why not set yourself a challenge every day to climb to the top of the stairs (whether at home or work), not only to prove your determination to reach the top, but also to improve aerobic health and bone mass?

All you need is a staircase of your choice – and if you find that once up to the top doesn't seem to be much effort, challenge yourself to gradually increase the climb or walk, to running up the stairs. Then, if you begin to find that too easy, repeat the run twice, then three times and so on.

Do this simple exercise every day to increase body strength and fitness levels and, of course, to give you a sense of Capricorn pride in your achievement.

Nutrition

Capricorn governs the bones and teeth, so foods that contain calcium – like dairy, sardines and dark, leafy greens – should be a regular part of your dietary plan. You are an authority on traditional dietary needs and are happy to tell all your friends and family that the tried-and-trusted route of 'moderation in all things' is the path to good health. But you don't always follow your own advice, and have secret food-scoffs and drink binges, particularly when you're under pressure from burning the metaphorical candle at both ends. (In the beauty section on p. 91, you will see how to burn a few candles to actually relax and restore your vitality.)

BREAKFAST BOOST

✳

Here's a thoroughly nourishing and delicious breakfast to set you up for the day. It includes classic ingredients to support Capricorn's love of traditional recipes.

You will need:
* 1 avocado, halved, peeled and mashed
* 1 tsp fresh lemon juice
* Tabasco, to taste
* 1 tbsp milk
* 4 eggs
* 1 tbsp chopped fresh chives, plus extra for garnish
* 1 tbsp unsalted butter
* 4 large, thin slices of rye bread
* 115g thinly sliced smoked salmon
* Sea salt and freshly ground black pepper, to taste

1. Place the mashed avocado in a bowl and add the lemon juice, freshly ground black pepper and Tabasco to taste.

2. Whisk the milk, eggs and tablespoon of chives in a large bowl.

3. Melt the butter in a pan, pour in the egg mixture and season with salt and pepper. Stir gently for about 3–4 minutes with a wooden spoon, turning the mixture each time it starts to stick to the bottom, until the eggs are scrambled. Remove from the heat.

4. Spread the mashed avocado over the slices of bread and spoon the scrambled eggs over the the top.

5. Drape a salmon slice over each open sandwich, and garnish with the remaining chives. Season again, to taste.

Enjoy starting off your working day with this protein-packed, carb-light energy booster.

....

GOAT'S CHEESE SNACK

✳

Calcium helps support Capricorn-ruled bones, and goat's milk is a very rich source. Here's a quick snack, taking only minutes to make, that you can pop into your backpack for when you're out on long country walks or bike rides.

You will need:
* 115g goat's cheese
* A little cream cheese, to taste
* A sprinkling of chopped rosemary leaves
* 60g chopped beetroot
* A few chopped walnuts
* 4 vine leaves, drained and rinsed (they are usually bought in a jar)

1. In a bowl, mix the goat's cheese, cream cheese and rosemary together.

2. Add the beetroot and walnuts and mix to combine.

3. Place spoonfuls of the mixture on the vine leaves, then roll them up.

4. Chill in the fridge for an hour in a storage box.

Don't forget to take your snack box with you when you set off on your travels.

Beauty

Business matters to the Goat, and so does making money. And if they don't already own shares in the perfume, flower or luxury industries, then investing in the beauty industry is likely to be on their to-do list for the future.

As every Capricorn knows, all the best facial spas, jade rollers, body soaps and mud baths are essential beauty accessories. In fact, the Goat is likely to have researched, tested and organised their own make-up and beauty routine into a highly structured and practical system. Here are just a couple of ideas for you to work into your well-honed daily regime.

....

LUNAR BATH RITUAL

♡

Every full moon, invest in this bath-time ritual to relax and beautify your inner soul, while helping you to clarify your Capricorn goals. The addition of the crystals to represent the four elements will also attract the worldly success you so deserve.

You will need:

* 1 malachite
* 1 citrine
* 1 red sunstone
* 1 blue lace agate
* 4 green tea lights
* A cup of Epsom salts
* 2 tsp bergamot essential oil
* 2 tsp sandalwood essential oil

1. Place a crystal and a tea light at each corner of the bath.

2. Add all the remaining ingredients to your bath.

3. As you soak and relax, focus on your personal mission statement: 'I will be successful in all I do, and I call on the moon to bring me the power to be so'.

Repeat this practice every full moon to align your own personal power, beautify your inner self and manifest success.

. . . .

SENSUAL MASSAGE

♡

Now, if you never indulge in a massage, you are not being true to your earthy self. Either find yourself a reputable massage therapist or aromatherapist and make it a regular event, or, if you have a partner or good friend, ask them to do this simple back massage for you.

You will need:
* 4 tsp almond oil
* 2 drops of sandalwood essential oil
* 4 drops of lavender essential oil
* 2 drops of lemon verbena essential oil

1. Lie on your front and ask your massage therapist to drizzle a little of the oil down your spine.

2. Ask them to gently knead your spine from the top, down to the coccyx or tailbone, then back up again.

3. Next, ask them to follow the same vertical direction of the spine, but this time with a little more pressure and with circular finger movements.

4. Finally, get them to use both techniques on your shoulders, moving slowly down both sides of the torso, until your whole back has been massaged.

5. Ask them to finish with gently percussive strokes from the sides of the hand all over the back.

6. Enjoy a cup of green tea together with your massage therapist, or anything else you fancy!

This massage will improve the nerve function of your spinal cord, while easing tension and benefitting the whole body.

CHAKRA BALANCE

The body's chakras are the epicentres of the life-force energy that flows through all things (see p. 20).

Capricorn is traditionally linked to the base chakra, located at the base of the spine, centred between the last disc at the back and the pubic bone to the front. This chakra is concerned with a sense of being 'grounded'. It provides a firm base and sense of security, plus it controls the basic functioning needs of the body. Capricorn is also associated with bones and joints. So a good way to determine whether your chakra is out of balance is to review the state of your joints, particularly the knees.

Flexible knee joints mean you have a flexible approach to life and your chakra is in balance. Stiff or creaky? You need to be more open to change and accept that life holds no guarantees.

If you have an underactive base chakra, your knees may feel weak or you stumble frequently. Mentally, you can't trust anyone, and so may be unable to get any project under way or finished. You also don't have the stamina to

get yourself motivated to do anything. To reinforce the base
chakra, wear or carry red carnelian, ruby or garnet. These stones will enhance motivation, release you from fears and self-doubt and enable you to trust in yourself and others (and you'll no longer go weak at the knees at the sight of a possible new romance, but stand firm and trust in your desires!).

An overactive base chakra results in you trying to dominate and control everyone; you may be pushy and fanatical about your goals, to such an extent that you try to bend everyone's will to your way. To subdue an overactive base chakra, wear or carry moonstone. It will make you more sensitive to the world around you, while calming down your controlling nature.

General Wellbeing

The wellbeing of the Capricorn body depends a lot on how well their mind is operating, and whether they are achieving their goals, or at least on the right pathway. However, in the world of enterprise, initiative and the road to success, you need to feel protected from negativity. The practices here will complement your already established body self-care routines, revive and vitalise your stylish potential and make sure that wherever you go, you are protected from environmental stress and negativity.

DUST IT OFF

The Goat's main focus in life is often to accomplish something for themselves that makes a statement in the outside world. This means they are frequently in contact with a wide range of people through their career or professional interests, so it's hardly surprising they are exposed to a lot of psychic energy – some good, but also some bad.

To shake off any negative or unwanted psychic debris, perform this practice at least once a week, if you can. You will need to get outside to do this one.

1. Stand outside in the garden, the countryside or another green space and raise your face to the clouds and skies.

2. If it's windy, face into the wind; if it's really sunny, make sure you don't look at the sun directly; if it's raining, start with an umbrella, then put it to one side as you raise your face to the rain.

3. Turn to the north and say, 'From this direction all bad intentions are gone'; turn to the south and say, 'From this direction all stress is removed'; turn to the east and say, 'I am cleansed and purified of all psychic pollution'; and turn to the west and say, 'I am free to move on, surrounded by my own positive energy'.

After this, you will feel cleansed of negativity, blessed with positivity and ready to get cracking with the best ways in which to achieve your aims.

CRYSTAL PROTECTION IN THE HOME

For all their business acumen, the Goat takes pride in their home, making sure everything is organised and in its rightful place. You may even be one of those Capricorns who loves a good declutter on a regular basis. Yet maybe there's one thing you haven't considered – and that's to protect your home from invisible negative energies using the power of your sun-sign crystal: ruby. Negative vibes come not only from people, but also from environmental influences, such as electric pylons, underground water courses, cables and light pollution.

Here's a simple remedy – to be performed preferably during a new-moon phase – to protect and attract positive, harmonious energy to your home.

You will need:
* A sage smudging stick
* 5 pieces of rough ruby
* A small bowl made of a natural material (wood, glass or china) of your choice

1. Light the smudging stick, until it smoulders.

2. Wave and waft the energy in all areas of your home, even in cupboards, bathrooms, sheds and so on. As you do so, imagine you are banishing, cleansing and removing negativity and replacing it with goodness.

3. Next, put the rubies in your bowl and place it at your main entrance, in a discreet or hidden position, so it won't be moved or touched by anyone (either on a high ledge or even under a piece of furniture – you don't have to see it for this to work).

Your home will now be blessed and protected from all forms of unwanted energy.

PART THREE
Caring For Your Soul

It is not because things are difficult that we do not dare; it is because we do not dare that they are difficult.

Seneca, Roman philosopher

This final section offers you tailored, fun, easy and amazing ways to connect to and care for your sacred self. This, in turn, means you will begin to feel at one with the joyous energy of the Universe. You don't have to sign up to any religion or belief system (unless you want to) – just take some time to experience uplifting moments through your interaction with the spiritual aspects of the cosmos. Care for your sun sign's soul centre, and you care about the Universe, too.

At the beginning of this book, we touched on the almost mystical aspect of the more ancient symbol of the Sea Goat (half goat, half fish) and how this represents both success born of practical wisdom and esoteric insight. And when it comes to spiritual belief systems, Capricorns tend either to dogmatically avoid all forms of spiritual belief, religion or pagan magic, because they're not 'real' or 'proven', or are secretly fascinated by them. To motivate that serious soul of yours, if you're not already doing so, read widely on a range of traditional beliefs, such as Eastern religions and philosophies, mystical traditions (for example, Kabbalah) or magical practices like Wicca.

Meanwhile, here are several practices you can enjoy to connect you to your own sacred self and its place in the Universe.

....

WINTER SOLSTICE RITUAL

✳

The day the sun moves into Capricorn marks the winter solstice in the northern hemisphere. This is the shortest day of light and has been a pivotal day in many spiritual traditions, marking the darkest moments of winter, followed by the rebirth of the sun as it begins to climb slowly again in the sky, towards its highest point.

The winter solstice was honoured by ancient peoples for its sacred significance and spiritual power as a turning point in the year. The practice below will help you with a turning point of your own – rather like stepping across a boundary, you will connect to your sacred self for a more fulfilling lifestyle.

Having said that, you don't have to wait until the solstice to perform this simple ritual because as a Capricorn, you're privileged to be born into solstice time and to carry the energy of this transformative period with you.

You will need:
* A garnet, ruby or obsidian
* A 90cm (36 inch) length of string, rope, twine or even ribbon

1. Lay the rope out in a horizontal line before you.

2. Hold the stone close to your belly and say the following out loud: 'As the sun changes from the dark of winter to the growth of light, so I cross the line from my own tangible self to my spiritual self'.

3. Close your eyes and really believe this affirmation as you say it.

4. Take one step over the rope, so that you are straddling the line, with one foot behind and one foot in front. Remain in this position for one minute and repeat the affirmation.

5. Next, take your back foot off the ground and place it beside the other. You have now moved from awareness of a physical presence to a new sense of the sacred within you.

6. As you say the following and final affirmation, move the stone close to the centre of your forehead (your third-eye chakra) and say: 'I have crossed the line and I believe in my sacred self'.

From now on, you will be more aware of your spiritual self, and how, when aligned with your material ambitions, it can bring you the kind of fulfilment you seek.

....

THE WEALTH OF THE UNIVERSE

♡

Once Capricorns have their minds set on what they really want to achieve, nothing much can stop them. But this spiritual exercise will enable you to connect to the creative force of the Universe to help you manifest it. It won't take long – maybe three to five minutes – and the more you practise it (say, once a week), the more likely you will plug into the cosmic energy and feel at one with the unlimited power of creativity.

1. Find a quiet place and sit comfortably – if possible, surrounded by Nature to enhance your connection to the force that flows through all things.

2. Let the natural world instil a sense of peace within you before you begin.

3. Close your eyes and let your mind drift. Notice how your mind fills with many thoughts – some good, some bad, some silly, some impossible. Be aware of how they come and go; observe them as if they were a bunch of intruders, gatecrashing your party.

4. Now empty your mind. This is challenging because the gatecrashers just keep coming back. But you're going to be a bit of a bouncer now: try a simple technique of counting slowly to 20 in your head and focus your mind on each number; then, if a rogue thought tries to muscle in on your party, bounce back to number 1 and start again.

5. Soon, you will find the intrusive thoughts go away and a sense of universal energy flows through you.

Persevere with this practice, until creative inspiration or sudden flashes of insight arise from a deep place within, and use these spiritual insights to shape your future.

SATOR SQUARE

★⋆
★

To promote Capricorns' need for some form of structured, mystical contemplation, this palindromic magic square is the perfect visual image to uplift you and stir your divine self. The Sator Square is believed by many experts to be a mystical or magical text first found in the ruins of Pompeii in southern Italy. No one really knows what it means, but it's long been used as a profound, esoteric magic text to promote a connection to the mysterious nature of oneself.

You will need:
* A piece of paper and a pen
* A candle for atmosphere

1. Write a word square with the following words:
SATOR
AREPO
TENET
OPERA
ROTAS

2. Light the candle, and gaze for a while at the words, reading them in whichever order you prefer – back to front, bottom to top, repeating them aloud or in your head, over and over again, like a mantra.

3. Now gaze into the candle flame and continue to repeat the mantra.

As you learn the words off by heart, you will begin to find them meaningless, but like any mantra, when repeated they open you up to another layer of consciousness, and one that leads to the deeper levels of self.

Place your Sator Square on a wall, leave it in a dedicated space or just chant the mantra aloud whenever you need to open up to mystery. Spiritual awareness can not only seed great ideas, but can also lead you to fantastic, uplifting achievements.

Last Words

The strange symbol of the Sea Goat (as described on p. 41) embodies both the instinctual wisdom of ancient magicians and the more materialistic viewpoint of a pragmatist. If you can harness both these energies and use them to your advantage, then the world becomes not so much a personal challenge, but a personal success. Self-care for Capricorn is about nurturing both of these sides of your nature, and realising that by caring for them both, you can get to where you truly want to be.

In this book, you have seen how to care for and promote your amazing determination. You have realised that your gritty quest for ambition is fuelled by your vulnerabilities and that love is not to be feared but is a never-ending exchange of respect and mutual acceptance. You also know that your image and physique are important symbols of your status, goals and ambition, and that inner beauty can be the best way to express this in your outer appearance.

The spiritual 'fish-tail' of the Sea Goat may be a

slippery, slightly niggling quality to accept in your practical world, but now you can begin to make use of that deeper instinct and bring your hidden sun-sign potentials to life. The practices in the book have shown you that self-care is more than just looking after your body; it's a holistic nurturing of mind, body and soul, and if you take the plunge and trust the process, you will be true to your authentic self. By enhancing your desire for success, caring about self-respect and becoming less controlling and simply trusting in others, you will be able to love who you are becoming.

Never give up on those Capricorn goals, because if you are going to dream, you might as well dream big. And remember – your character is your destiny.

Resources

Main sites for crystals, stones, candles, smudging sticks, incense, pouches, essential oils and everything needed for the holistic self-care practices included in this book:

holisticshop.co.uk
thepsychictree.co.uk
thesoulangels.co.uk
earthcrystals.com
livrocks.com
artisanaromatics.com

For a substantial range of books (and metaphysical items) on astrology, divination, runes, palmistry, tarot and holistic health, etc.:

thelondonastrologyshop.com
watkinsbooks.com
mysteries.co.uk
barnesandnoble.com
innertraditions.com

For more information on astrology, personal horo-
scopes and birth-chart calculations:
astro-charts.com (simplest, very user friendly)

horoscopes.astro-seek.com
(straightforward)
astrolibrary.org/free-birth-chart
(easy to use, with lots of extra information)

Glossary

Aura An invisible electromagnetic energy field that emanates from and surrounds all living beings

Auric power The dominant colour of the aura that reveals your current mood or state

Chakra Sanskrit for 'wheel', in Eastern spiritual traditions the seven chakras are the main epicentres – or wheels – of invisible energy throughout the body

Dark of the moon This is when the moon is invisible to us, due to its proximity to the sun; it is a time for reflection, solitude and a deeper awareness of oneself

Divination Gaining insight into the past, present and future using symbolic or esoteric means

Double-terminator crystal A quartz crystal with a point at each end, allowing its energy to flow both ways

Full moon The sun is at its maximum opposition to the moon, thus casting light across all of the moon's orb; in esoteric terms, it is a time for culmination, finalising deals, committing to love and so on

Geopathic stress Negative energy emanating from and on the Earth, such as underground water courses, tunnels, overhead electrical cables and geological faults

Grid A specific pattern or layout of items symbolising specific intentions or desires

Horoscope An astrological chart or diagram showing the position of the sun, moon and planets at the time of any given event, such as the moment of somebody's birth, a marriage or the creation of an enterprise; it is used to interpret the characteristics or to forecast the future of that person or event

New crescent moon A fine sliver of crescent light that appears curving outwards to the right in the northern hemisphere and to the left in the southern hemisphere; this phase is for beginning new projects, new romance, ideas and so on

Psychic energy One's intuition, sixth sense or instincts, as well as the divine, numinous or magical power that flows through everything

Shadow side In astrology, your shadow side describes those aspects of your personality associated with your opposite sign and of which you are not usually aware

Smudging Clearing negative energy from the home with a smouldering bunch of dried herbs, such as sage

Solar return salutation A way to give thanks and welcome the sun's return to your zodiac sign once a year (your birthday month)

Sun in opposition The sun as it moves through the opposite sign to your own sun sign

Sun sign The zodiac sign through which the sun was moving at the exact moment of your birth

Waning moon The phase of the moon after it is full, when it begins to lose its luminosity – the waning moon is illuminated on its left side in the northern hemisphere, and on its right side in the southern hemisphere; this is a time for letting go, acceptance and preparing to start again

Waxing moon The phase between a new and a full moon, when it grows in luminosity – the waxing moon is illuminated on its right side in the northern hemisphere and on its left side in the southern hemisphere; this is a time for putting ideas and desires into practice

Zodiac The band of sky divided into twelve segments (known as the astrological signs), along which the paths of the sun, the moon and the planets appear to move

About the Author

After studying at the Faculty of Astrological Studies in London, the UK, Sarah gained the Diploma in Psychological Astrology – an in-depth 3-year professional training programme cross-fertilised by the fields of astrology and depth, humanistic and transpersonal psychology. She has worked extensively in the media as astrologer for titles such as *Cosmopolitan* magazine (UK), *SHE, Spirit & Destiny* and the *London Evening Standard*, and appeared on UK TV and radio shows, including *Steve Wright in the Afternoon* on BBC Radio 2.

Her mainstream mind-body-spirit books include the international bestsellers, *The Tarot Bible, The Little Book of Practical Magic* and *Secrets of the Universe in 100 Symbols*. .

Sarah currently practises and teaches astrology and other esoteric arts in the heart of the countryside.

Acknowledgements

I would first like to thank everyone at Yellow Kite, Hodder & Stoughton and Hachette UK who were part of the process of creating this series of twelve zodiac self-care books. I am especially grateful to Carolyn Thorne for the opportunity to write these guides; Anne Newman for her editorial advice, which kept me 'carefully' on the right track; and Olivia Nightingall who kept me on target for everything else! It is when people come together with their different skills and talents that the best books are made – so I am truly grateful for being part of this team.

See the full Astrology Self-Care series here

9781399704885   9781399704915   9781399704588

9781399704618   9781399704649   9781399704670

9781399704700 9781399704731 9781399704762

9781399704793 9781399704823 9781399704854

yellow
kite

books to help you live a good life

Join the conversation and tell
us how you live a #goodlife

🐦 @yellowkitebooks
📘 YellowKiteBooks
📌 Yellow Kite Books
📷 YellowKiteBooks